THOUGHTS AND TIME

W. Dutchak (Wladicus)
(c) 2013

First Printing .... June 2013
Second Printing .... August 2014

ISBN: 978-0-9693199-5-5

Thoughts and Time

by W. Dutchak

Copyright 2013

by W. Dutchak

* * * *

by Walter Dutchak
Part 1 – Thoughts and Time (c) 2001 & 2013
Part 2 – Attitude for Change (c) 1987 & 2013

by Rose -Marie Dutchak (Borowsky)
Part 3 – My Yesterday (c) 2001 & 2013

* * * *

SECTION NOTES

This work / book is compiled into three (3)
different sections as follows:

SECTON 1:   Thoughts and Time

This section is a collection of meditations, thoughts,
ideas and song lyrics written in poetry form
by the author – from 1967 until 2011.

SECTON 2: Attitude for Change

This section records a talk given to a group
of people who meet to share their understanding of life
and learn about going beyond fixed concepts.

The talk discusses attitudes and perception that
can open one to experience life
from a different perspective.

WALT DUTCHAK

~_~_~_~_~_~

SECTION NOTES (continued)

SECTON 3:   My Yesterday

This section features the lyrics to songs
written by Rose-Marie Borowsky
from 1966 to 1977.

ROSE-MARIE DUTCHAK

Each section is a reflection of the authors' personal
journeys in, relationship to, and understanding of life.

~_~_~_~_~
\\\\\\\\\\\\

TABLE of CONTENTS

SECTION NOTES iii

Section 1 - THOUGHTS AND TIME 1

A Cosmic Bliss 30

A Universe of Memories 33

A 25

ALWAYS 57

Ancient Dreams 55

B 25

Come Again 9

CONFUSION 3

ELECTRIFIED 29

Few There Are 27

Flight of the Eagle 51

Fly Around 23

For Love A Life 11

F-R-A-G-M-E-N-T-S   (1)................................. 37

F-R-A-G-M-E-N-T-S   (2)................................. 42

F-R-A-G-M-E-N-T-S   (3)................................. 45

Happy Heart 5

March 16, 1987 44

Melody of Love 8

Once I Was A Sailor 28

People Running People Down 16

RAIN DOES DROP 13

Self Reflection 5

Smiling Eyes 50

Tell Me Why 20

That You Care 14

That's Life 6

The Light of Joy 59

The Realm of Reality 4

The Spring of Life 12

The Way I Think of You 18

There Are Wonders 26

They Didn't Know 15

Thoughts And Time 22

Time and Now 32

To Keet 34

W A T E R 31

What A Sight 24

Wings of Freedom 10

WINGS of FREEDOM ~ 2 48

Y O U 53

Your Struggling Soul 2

Section 2 - ATTITUDE for CHANGE 60

Opening Words 61

Introduction to "ATTITUDE for CHANGE" 68

*** ATTITUDE for CHANGE *** 70

CONDITIONED THINKING 73

DIE BEFORE YOU DIE 77

THE PLACE OF THOUGHT 80

BEYOND THOUGHT-PERCEPTION 85

TO BE OR NOT TO BE 90

BEYOND CONCEPTUAL REALITY 92

LOVE HAS NO OPPOSITE 94

COMMUNICATING

the ATTITUDE for CHANGE 98

AS TO THE CHANGE 100

KNOW THYSELF 103

Section 3 - My Yesterday 107

A Friend of Mine 128
ALWAYS 125
ARE YOU ? 129
Blue-Green Mountain 124
Cold Like the Wind 112
Did You Ever ? 116
Happiness My Way 119
I Love Thee 111
Is It Love? 115
It Came Naturally 120
My Yesterday 121
Recipe for Happiness 118
REMEMBERING MEMORIES 108
Rippling Waters 122
Sands of Yesterday 117
SUMMER SOUNDS 110
That's Life 123
The Secret of Life 113
To Be Free 126
What's the Use of Living 114
When Will We Ever Learn 127

Wladicus

2013.05.25
and 2014.08.23

Section 1
Thoughts and Time

This section is a collection of thoughts, meditations, and
songs
written in poetic form since 1967.
Below each title I have shown the original
date of writing

I have found that poetry, or the poetic form of expressing
thoughts, seems to convey so much more than prose
could ever expect to. Poetry is dynamic – it is never the
same. Depending on your mood, your feelings and your
insight, it may convey different images on different
occasions.

I will not even attempt to explain the poetry. Its rightful
meaning will be that which you perceive every time that
you read it. The collection poems towards the end of this
section called 'FRAGMENTS' (1), (2) and (3) was so
named because these fragments represent pieces of a
whole picture. Our lives are made up of such fragments,
and perhaps it would be to our advantage to review these
fragments more often, and see how they are actually an
integral part of life and not events that appear to separate
and isolate us from the wholeness we all seek. In
meditation fragments are integrated into a wholeness
that can help to clarify our limited understanding of life.

~ wladicus ~

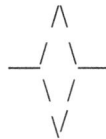

1

Your Struggling Soul

= *October 1967* =
(Lyrics to a song)

Where is the world of love, of truth
and of joy?
Why can't the souls of earthly people
understand?
Are we to be doomed, because our
minds destroy
The meaning of brotherly love
our spirits demand?

Our lonely hearts – wander –
through the roads of fear,
The fear of truth, the truth that
ignorance can hide.

Let your soul reach out,
and then the meaning will be clear.
The truth is there, but your spirit
must be the guide.

Your struggling soul endures
many hard lives
Before the light of truth – comes
clearly through.
And when your spirit understands
the wonders in the skies –
Then brotherly love, and truth,
will come to you.

wladicus – 1967.10

CONFUSION

= November 1, 1967 =

It is very nice to know
that you exist like so.
But do you ever stop to think
what a puzzled world this is,
And how each element
seems so unique?

Have a good look about you,
then try to reason if
this is madness,
Or a logic absurd.

We ironically think we see the unseen
and know the unknown –
The obvious is not obvious
when our minds over magnify
Things of insignificance.

To think that we know the unknown,
is to enter a free-fall
Through endless confusion.

wladicus – 1967.11.01

The Realm of Reality

= *January 12, 1968* =

Inspirational thoughts of galaxies unknown
Await reception by mankind, yearning alone.

Man looks for an answer, to grasp, and clutch,
within his hands,
Within his mind, his consciousness, his vision,
his dream.

Reality is just the grasp beyond;
that which is there, and yet, unseen.
And to feel its presence is to hear
the whisper in the wind,
Or the moment of stillness, which grows
with anticipation,
But escapes understanding, and reason.

You cannot touch reality,
you cannot hear it nor see it.
You must know it, and feel it
with the arms of your soul.

True reality is a reality beyond reality,
and so real, that to us
It becomes unreality, seemingly a wish
of mystical utopia.

—·—

Happy Heart

= February 2, 1968 =

Just be honest in every way,
Live the fullest every day.
May your heart be happy and gay,
at school, at work, at play.

-*-

Self Reflection

= June 25, 1968 =

Cans't thou see that what
becomes of thine own self
reflecteth upon the image of
thy brothers?

~/\~

That's Life

= *May 10, 1968* =

Born into a world unknown,
we are what it makes us,
and after childhood, supposedly,
adulthood;
Yet sometimes with doubt –
we mold our lives, if not,
our lives are molded for us by that
which surrounds us,
although we sometimes think
that we control it.

There comes a time, in young adolescence,
when feelings are strange and daring;
Of pleasure, of joy, of happiness
and wonder.

Beauty and grace, tenderness, warmth,
Love and fancy, envelope the thoughts
Of minds, which are ripe and ready,
to reap the riches of life.

But sometimes, all too soon,
devotion and understanding become
meaningless, worthless, deceiving.
And treacherous roads, with blasphemy,
echo words of righteousness,
In struggling moments of misguided beings.

Where before there was but warmth,
there now is a cold, glaring stare of rage.

continued ...

As endless time goes by,
the years of graying hair creep in,
And the moods of quarreling slip into
oblivion.
Expressions of wisdom, subdue all
selfishness,
And the calamity of heated fury – subsides.

Now comes and understanding for the worth
of that which was worthless.

And yet, in aging, there occurs a
rejuvenation,
A reunion with the whims of love,
and a new gaiety, that begs for
Another embrace with the years that youth
alone can know.

But it is now not far, when relaxing and
reflecting will fill the hours with saged
Thoughts of a life – in a life,
where life is understood
when life becomes no more,
to start again.

_x_

Melody of Love

= June 4, 1968 =
(Lyrics to a song)

The sun streaks down from the heavens above;
The moon gleams brightly for lovers in love;
The woods grow shrubs and flowers, and trees,
While ever-loving birds, chirp their melodies.

For every smile, the sun shines stronger;
For every kiss, the moon glows longer;
From every flower comes the buzz of a bee;
From every tree, an ever-loving melody.

With a radiant smile, our love grows stronger;
As the moon shines on, our joy lasts longer.
The flowers are fragrant, and the honey is sweet,
And the melody is love, from a dear heart-beat.

--X--

Come Again

= *July 25, 1968* =
(Lyrics to a song - tango)

Come again,
Come my love,
Come again to me.

I have thoughts of thee,
Sacred thoughts to me;
Of love, of joy, of warmth –
I see what it could be.

Come and see me now,
I'm sure I've changed somehow;
I know that I was no
At peace – my mind, a cloud.

Come my love to me,
Can it really be?
But it was just a dream I had –
I sit, and cry, a plead.

Come again,
Come my love,
Come again to me.

_-<>-_

Wings of Freedom

= *July 28,1968* =
(Lyrics to a song)

High up in the sky the birds do fly,
They spread their wings, and soar and dive.

Down on the ground, where people are found,
The birds do fear to come around.

Why do they fear so much to come,
And see us down upon the ground?

Maybe the answer is there for me;
I look up in the sky, and there I see –

The birds do fly, and soar around,
On wings of freedom, they leave the ground.

But men have flown; they reached the sky
On silvered wings, and still they died.

And still they look, and search the skies
For wings of freedom, to leave the ground.

But why must they try to leave the ground,
When freedom for men, on earth must be found?

Wings of freedom are to the birds,
Who fly up in the sky ...

~~o~~

For Love A Life

= *February 12, 1969* =
(Lyrics to a song)

The time has come,
And love someone I must,
For in the end
All turns to dust.

And life is bright,
So full of delight;
The world is quite
A wonderful sight –

Tonight ...

What a wonderful inspiration
for life – for life;

And love someone – I must,
Live – for love a life.

The time has come,
And life is bright,
A wonderful sight –

Tonight ...

...?...

The Spring of Life

= *March 21, 1969 (1:00 am)* =
(Lyrics to a song)

Listen to the breathing woods,
In the golden mist
of an early evening shower;
Spongy ground beneath my feet,
And living air surrounds
the first spring hour.

Silver drops from a sun-glazed cloud,
Race towards fields
that must be plowed.
The hiding sun in crimson splendor,
Warms young hearts that sing out loud.

The wind still wet, the night grows cold,
And moving darkness hides
the rainbow's crest;
Rosy days of warmth and beauty –
All life awaits to spring
from nature's breast.

Listen to the breathing woods,
Spongy ground beneath my feet;
Silver drops from a sun-glazed cloud,
And fields, that must be plowed.

_()_

RAIN DOES DROP

= *April 23, 1969* =
(A simple example for my grade 7 student's poetry lesson)

Piddle-paddle, pipple-plop,
Oh so gently rain does drop.
Rain does drop? Oh, rain does drop.
Yes, the rain does drop.

Swish-swash, wishee-wash,
Wipers wash and people rush.
Rain does drop? Oh, rain does drop.
Yes, the rain does drop.

Splish-splash, people dash,
Lightning flash, thundering crash.
Wham-bam, doors do slam,
Shutters open, windows jam.

Drip-drop, leaky top,
Trickles down and fills the pot.
Piddle-paddle, pipple-plop,
Oh so gently rain does drop.

__//__

That You Care

= July 27, 1969 =
(Lyrics to a song)

Now that you know me,
How can you show me
That you care ?

The world goes **ZING !**
The world goes
Ting-a-ling-a-ding-a-ring-a-dare,
I don't care, I don't care !

Stay right beside me,
Always remind me
That you care.

Eyes up to the sky,
Eyes up, never
Do-a-ding-a-dang-a-down,
Look around, look around !

Life is **ZIP !**
Life is like a little
Dip-a-whip-a-flip,
What a trip, what a trip !

So now that you know me,
Stay right beside me;
And always remind me,
That you care.

—\/\/—

They Didn't Know

= *July 31, 1969* =
(Lyrics to a song)

Once upon a time not long ago,
The woods then did sing, the winds did blow,
Upon this Earth, they didn't know.

To know is better than not to know,
I know it's better than not to know.

Alive, strong and free, with twinkling eyes,
The breed of all mankind, beneath virgin skies;
What was to come, they didn't know

The years went on by, and man did learn
The secrets of life, and things of no concern;
All that of what, they didn't know.

To know is better than not to know,
But not to know is better than not to know;

And man tried to show all that he knew.
Power was there for man to use;
And by knowing, they didn't know.

The woods did not sing, the winds began to grow –
The skies were all dimmed, the sun didn't glow;
Oh what on Earth ! ... They didn't know.

Now is the time, the time of knowing.
The woods still do sing, the winds keep blowing;
Will someone say, they didn't know ?

To know is better than not to know,
But not to know is better than not to know;
not to know is better than not to know

-***-

People Running People Down

= *August 26, 1969* =
(Lyrics to a song)

All the time I look around,
People running people down.
The world goes spinning 'round and 'round,
People running people down.

People rush and many hurry,
Some do push and others worry.
The world does spinning 'round and 'round,
People running people down.

All you people look around,
Stop your silly running around.
People running all around,
People running people down.

*Find yourself, come on out
Of that crowd rushing about;
People realize what you do,
They are wise – those who do.*

All you people seeking wealth,
Do you really know yourself ?
People running all around,
People running people down.

continued ...

People Running People Down (continued)…

STOP RIGHT THERE !
WHO ARE YOU
RUNNING AROUND,
AS YOU DO ?

People pushing in a hurry,
People rushing in a scurry,
People running all around,
People running people down.

(Repeat the first verse)

oOo

The Way I Think of You

= *August 28, 1969* =
(Lyrics to a song)

This is the way I think of you,
Twinkling stars and the morning dew,
Mountain streams clear and blue,
This is the way I think of you.

A new day starts when the sun comes up,
A father sighs when his son grows up.
Day to day no time is forlorn,
Day to day a life is born.

Streams where water lilies grow;
Silver valleys full of snow;
Giving life and giving rest,
Giving love and happiness.

Stars will shine both day and night,
The moon reflecting lover's light.
The evening dims and the morning dawns,
The baby cries and the mother comes.

continued …

Velvet petals spreading out
To the world 'round about,
Showing beauty and the color
Of a lovely country flower.

Setting suns and rising moons,
Summer nights and mellow tunes –
Loving just the one you love,
Loving for the sake of love.

Whispers in a gentle breeze,
Singing loving melodies.
Happy tear drops wetting cheeks,
Winding paths and trickling creeks.

This is the way I think of you ...
Think of you ...
Think of you ...

-///-

Tell Me Why

= *September 5, 1969* =
(Lyrics to a song)

Tell me why !
Why so many stars in the sky ?
Why do little babies cry ?
Tell me why ? –
Can you tell me why ?

How many people say,
Why do the priests all pray ?
How many girls sign,
Oh what a lovely guy ?

Why-oh-why ? – Can you tell me why ?

Why do the blossoms smell so good ?
Why does fire burn the wood ?
Can you tell me why ?

Can all the people sing ?
Why do the church bells ring ?
Why do the children run,
and have a lot of fun ?

Why-oh-why ? – Can you tell me why ?

continued …

Why is life so short I ask ?
Can there be another task ?

What would a wise man say –
Love on a lovely day ?
What does a gypsy feel ?
How many people steal ?

Tell me why !

Why are doves like angels white ?
Why so many brothers fight ?

To face the thing you fear,
How many people dare ?
To stand free and shout –
Is there a care, a doubt ?

Why-oh-why ? – Can you tell me why ?

Why do I sing this quizzing song ?
Tell me people, am I wrong ?

Why-oh-why ? – Can you tell me why ?

Tell me why !

_-*-_

Thoughts And Time

= October 18, 1969 =
(Lyrics to a song)

Floating thoughts in the air,
Autumn leaves, trees are bare.
Drifting down, swirling around,
Brown on yellow on red, no sound
Just dancing – the sky – the ground.

Coming or going, thoughts and time.

Floating thoughts in the air,
Memories wander, thoughts to share.
Breathe and breath, live and climb,
A breath, a thought, a place, a time ...
To think – life is a rhyme.

Coming or going, thoughts and time.

Floating thoughts in the air,
Floating thoughts, thoughts that care.
Drifting down, swirling around,
Brown on yellow on red, no sound
Just dancing – the sky – the ground.

-+-

Fly Around

= *November 30, 1969* =
(Lyrics to a song)

Sunny rays and shimmering sounds,
Dew drops melt – trickling down;
Run away the time – fly around.

Hazy days and golden dawns,
Dusty roads and carpet lawns;
Come awake, your mind – fly around.

Thinking and wondering,
Blinking and blundering,
Drinking and suffering,
Singing and offering –
Jump up high, and look – fly around.

Pretty girls and handsome boys,
Childish games – many toys;
Follow me, float away – fly around.

Flying like a butterfly,
Diving with an eagle's eye,
Soaring like a jet on high,
Exploring with a gasping sigh—
For a joy, just think – fly around.

Sunny rays and shimmering sounds,
Dew drops melt – trickling down;
Run away the time – fly around.

~~o~~

What A Sight

= *January 6, 1970* =
(Lyrics to a song)

I went to the town all alone,
Letting all my thoughts there to roam;
Nothing but a camera in my hand,
I stopped, and looked,
and saw the world stand.

CHORUS

What a sight ! My delight.
People talking here and there;
Some are rushing, some don't care:
Talking, walking, rushing, bending,
Stretching, pushing, and upending,
Yelling, telling, even selling,
Looking, chewing, eating, smelling –
What a sight ! My delight;
What a sight ! What a sight !

I said to myself standing there –
Look all around you, be aware.
Waiting with my camera for a chance,
I stopped, and looked,
and watched the world dance.

CHORUS

Do you know what I've got ?
Something priceless can't be bought.
Behind a camera moving fast,
I snapped, and caught
the moments as they passed.

CHORUS

= # =

A

= February 1970 =

Come and get some happiness,
Warmth and joy and friendliness.
Just forget the past behind –
Future brings a better time.

–·–

B

= February 1970 =

When I know the time is right,
That I may, that I might,
Fly to me my destiny,
The world is mine in eternity.

–:–

There Are Wonders

= *March 3, 1970* =

How should I tell you ?
Or should I only ask and not tell ?
But no doubt, not all can plainly see
for themselves;
There are wonders to be known.

The flowers bloom so beautifully,
Up to the skies they open.
The sun shines so richly –
Making golden a milky face.

We are looking at a treasure,
All life is like gold –
Budding life comes to a full bloom,
Winds do blow and sing a tune
Carrying thoughts to our minds.

A storm, a storm, thunder !
All is ruined ! All is deafened ...

Then the sun emerges ever glowing,
The wind has faded and stopped its blowing –
Surely, there are wonders to be known.

----}{----

Few There Are

= *May 1970* =

YOUTH IS CRYING;
PEOPLE WATCHING:
YOUTH IS ASKING,
BUT FEW THERE ARE
WHO GIVE A TRY.

MURKY RIVERS FLOWING BY,
BLACKENED SMOKE
FILLS THE SKY,
BUT FEW THERE ARE
WHO GIVE A TRY.

LIFE IS WATER,
LIFE IS AIR,
LIFE IS YOUTH,
IF WE CARE –
BUT FEW THERE ARE
WHO GIVE A TRY.

_!_

Once I Was A Sailor

= *October 7, 1970* =
(Lyrics to a song)

Once I was a sailor,
Crossed the ocean blue.
Came to a land –
A land I tell you,
'Twas a land
full of lovely life –
And there I tried to stay.

We dream of lands
across the seas;
Dreamy thoughts –
a mystic breeze.

When will I find this land again –
Lovely life where it all began ?

This land is beyond
the reach of seas,
The land within our memories.

Once you're a sailor
You sail for life,
And find that land
Of lovely life.

_+_/

ELECTRIFIED

= November 14, 1970 =

In this book you will find
Just words – or maybe what you seek.
To these thoughts I once was blind,
But now I see of what they speak.

Like through a fog, slowly clearing,
I begin to see, with each stride,
A truth ahead of me appearing;
To it, my mind electrified !

.../I\...

A Cosmic Bliss

= *November 19, 1970* =

My heart is light, on air does fly,
With vivid delight the soul does cry.

A cry of joy with bonds released,
A growing poise with love increased.

Increasing in range like vibrant tone,
Expressions change and reach the unknown.

Unknown yet known; for in your reach
A truth is sown, and this will teach.

Teach it will, and with such fairness,
As with a shrill – alights awareness.

Awareness is a truth, a light.
A cosmic bliss, a soul's delight.

,,,—,,,

WATER

= May 31, 1971 =

My palm, full of water, squeezes tight,
And my fingers press with the greatest might;
And then I look in this palm of mine,
My hand's all wet – but the water's fine.

The water cares not what you do to it,
For it will feed, it will cleanse,
There are many things
To which it lends.

And so you see, do as you please,
But lend yourself and be at ease.

Be like the water
That flows with glee,
And serve with faith,
Knowing that you are free.

Though the water flow may sometimes stop,
Rays of sunlight will raise it up.
And muddy water, and water marred by man,
Rises clean, and soon comes back –
To flow again.

oOo

Time and Now

= July 21, 1971 & 2001.09.02 =

The world before is the world now,
Breeding the world tomorrow somehow.
There is no time, no loan;
All is now – the timeless zone.

All that is physical manifests in time –
All that is thinking follows that line;
Thought is memories of happenings past;
Thought is hope for things to last.

Thought, sweet memory's mime,
Accumulating, coagulating – time;
A psychic illusion, a binding reality,
An escape from cosmic totality.

Released from memory's plow,
Reveling in the eternal now,
Unbound, unlimited, free of time;
Free of thought's babbling rhyme.

-xxx-

A Universe of Memories

= *March 11, 1972* =

Never did I look and see
All the beauty in a tree –

Never did I touch and feel,
Such a warmth that is real –

I look around and I can see
Things are happening to me –

Then I see things as they really be,
Full of life and harmony –

A world beyond the bounds of a sea,
A universe without end, in eternity –

Stretching out in galaxies,
A Universe of Memories.

~-~

To Keet

= *October 21, 1979* =

Kitty-cat, pussy-cat
Scruffy neck, bushy fur,
Layin' there as you purr –
Meoww !

Pussy-cat, kitty-cat,
Sitting snug, on my lap –
Gettin' set for a nap –
Meoww !

Do you care,
Does the world alarm you ?
No, you don't care,
Not a worry confounds you
'Cause – you're – a

Kitty –cat, pussy-cat,
Full of life – zip and zest.
THIS IS MY TIME TO REST –
Meoww !

Pussy-cat, kitty-cat,
Ears all perked, eyes so bright,
Playful paws – a child's delight –
Meoww !

_–-^-–_

Poet of the Heart

= October 29, 1985 =

A thought belabors his endless toil,
A poet at heart, a worker of soil –
The sky above, the earth below,
And space beyond with worlds to know.

What power guides, what secret lies
For man to find beyond the skies?
And wisdom sings a holy hymn –
The dawning skies are deep within.

Learned men do speak and tell
Of knowledge, and power as well.
And boldly they do proclaim
The countless virtues of the same!

But what of joy and what of beauty?
What of love, and what of duty?
Asleep, this inattentive lot
Who wander the cavities of thought!

continued …

What thought can remark
Beyond all amusement,
That joy is a spark –
And beauty its movement?

Can knowledge claim the throne above
With power as its deputy?
Can it displace the work of love
Where duty leads to harmony?

Behold, a wakeful poet of the heart,
A worker of soil, enacts his duty –
Joins the chorus and lives his part
In a song of joy, the symphony of beauty.

_=*=_

F-R-A-G-M-E-N-T-S (1)

= *March 11, 1987* =

We must not complicate the issue with laws upon laws
and rules upon rules...

We must learn to see beyond these limits.

Mental complexities are the product of a conceptual mind
weaving patterns with fixed concepts,
and the result is ultimate entanglement in that web.

And then, we have to continually refer
to those laws and rules
again and again,
to disentangle ourselves.

And so the process repeats in an endless cycle – until –
Until we clearly see – perceive –
what is actually happening.

Then the Chattering brain reveals itself.
It does no have the answer –
It has many answers – depending on the mood,
the environment,
and the stimuli presenting themselves.

A complete picture of mental fragmentation
becomes apparent.

continued ...

How can there be unity,
even a semblance of a wholesome life,
when the mind is totally fragmented
with a patchwork of complex concepts,
each one competing for prominence,
and each one, at the same time,
trying to figure out what the others are trying to say ?

In a quiet moment – sometimes –
just stop all activity – and observe the mind.

Don't interfere !
Just watch what it is doing.
The chatter that echoes
through that maze of "gray matter"
will astound you !

Out of this confusion must come order
before one can seriously consider anything else.

Can we see anger as it starts to move
through that mental maze ?
Then having spotted it, can we see
the consequences of expressing that anger
before it moves any further ?

continued …

Can we see the strings, the sutures,
that attach us,
and surgically bind us
to a concept, and idea, a feeling,
and make us one with that thing ?

Why must one be attached to anything ?
Do we enjoy being limited, and enslaved
to a mere idea, a concept ?

Surely, we have a potential to be greater than that !

Now if one is not careful,
here is where one falls into a trap.
Realizing that there is a disturbance, or disharmony,
one usually looks for the law, or rule
that will explain the governing principle.

That is to say, that one *assumes*
that there is a law or principle of action
for every problem situation,
and then one proceeds to apply some neat,
memorized formula
for guiding one back onto "the path".

It's nice and neat, and makes one feel good.
If, after a while, one approach hasn't worked,
then one tries another formula –
and so on – and so on – and so on.

continued ...

The problem here is that the formula is not permanent,
and neither is it dynamic.
It is fraught with limitations.
Every time the same sort of problem reappears
the same principle, or law, or rule, or whatever,
has to be applied again, and again.
And the battle continues,
even when one thinks that the problem has been solved.

What has happened,
is that one concept – the formula, or law, or rule,
has been applied to another concept
– the problem.

It is a battle of concepts that ensues,
and the fragmentation continues,
one concept trying to master another.

The mind is still chattering.
It has not been mastered.
One is still attached to ideas, to concepts,
to controlling principles and laws.
They are all concepts........

So, how does one escape such a dilemma ?

continued ...

As long as concepts of any sort
    are masters, or the motivators,
    the controlling factors in life,
then we are attached to them by implication,
they being our possessions,
and we, in reciprocation, being their slaves.

That is being enslaved to one's own possessions
    to the point where the possession
    and the possessor are indistinguishable.

They are one and the same thing.

If you are angry
then you *are* anger.

_###_

F-R-A-G-M-E-N-T-S (2)

= March 14, 1987 =

Simplicity !

Make it simple Walt,
  make it simple.

Thought oh thought,
  where have you gone ?
Thought oh thought,
  can you undo −
what you have done ?

"I think, therefore I am",
  said the philosopher.
And what then does that make me ?

The distinction between a fool and a wise man
    lies in their awareness.
The one thinks that he knows,
      and the other
    knows that he thinks !

The one that thinks that he knows
    has another think coming.
He can think and think,
    and think some more.

continued ...

And there are always things to think about.
And the more he thinks,
the more he thinks he knows,
and deeper, and deeper into the trap
he goes.

But, the one who knows that he thinks
also knows the value of thinking
and its place.

He does not permit
undue importance to thoughts,
because he sees them for what they are.
He sees how they function,
and how they should be used.

He is the master
and thoughts are his tools,
to calculate, to formulate and to communicate.

He sees clearly
that thoughts must not be permitted
to make the man, but
that the man must orchestrate the thoughts
for purposeful and harmonious manifestation.

A fool values a thought
while a wise man
sees the value of a thought.

continued ...

The one who values a thought
becomes so attached to it
that he cannot easily part with it.

It becomes a fixation, and a motivating factor
for a chain of causation,
the effects of which are most difficult to escape.

But, the one who sees the value of a thought
knows when, and how to use it,
and he knows also when it is fruitless
and not worthy of consideration.

oOo

March 16, 1987

*Don't say
"The sky's the limit"
for I have been there
and saw that it is not.*

*If there is a limit
then I know it not.*

_.|._

F-R-A-G-M-E-N-T-S (3)

= March 24, 1987 =

CALAMITY, you are a devious nature.
You entice, you enslave.
You press so incessantly and confuse the soul.

Can you not see that we have had enough of you,
and need no more ?

You are no mystery to me.
I see you in your feigned innocence,
as you start to prowl the chambers of thought.

You present arguments and excuses
to justify your existence.
You tell me that I cannot live without you.

BUT I DO NOT BUY THAT !

I can see that you are the offspring of your ancestors.
Your antiquity is obvious, and now
what purpose you may have had,
has come to an end.

You thought that you could find a dwelling place in me –
to build your pride, and increase your stature,
and shout out "This is the way it should be !"

continued …

Your world is not for me.
I parted company with you,
and now I am free.

And now that I see you for what you are,
You shake and tremble,
revealed before my piercing glare.

And then you fade away
in hopes of appearing on a better day.
But your hope is limited
and cannot grasp the way I go.

Calamity, your work is done with me !
I have changed
and am not what I was before.

"Change !", you shout.
"I can change !", you pretend.
But this change
you will never comprehend.

You and your brothers are a mischievous lot.
You offer false hopes and stir up desires.
Your change is directed by what was before,
which is more of the same in another decor.

continued …

Time is your hope, and
time is your limit.
Your days are numbered, and in time
you are finished !

There is a source that is beyond the realm of time.
It declares no limit;
and for you, it will always be undefined.

Oh, Calamity ! I know you well.
No longer do I feel your sting:
You have been totally disarmed,
and all that remains is a shell.

Your selfish nature has been revealed,
and soon others will know –
There is another way, a different world –
A place where you cannot go.

oOo

WINGS of FREEDOM ~ 2

= October 23, 1987 =
(Revised with additional lyrics to a song)

=CHORUS=:

High up in the sky
the birds do fly,
They spread their wings,
and soar and dive.

Down on the ground,
where people are found,
The birds do fear
to come around.

1. Why do they fear so much to come,
   And see us down upon the ground?
   Maybe the answer is there for me;
   I look up in the sky, and there I see –
   The birds do fly, and soar around,
On wings of freedom, they leave the ground.

   =CHORUS=: . . . High up in the sky ...

2. But men have flown; they reached the sky
   On silvered wings, and still they died.
   And still they look, and search the skies
For wings of freedom, to leave the ground.
   But wings of freedom are to the birds,
   Who fly up in the sky...

continued ...

=CHORUS=: . . . High up in the sky ...

3. But why must they try to leave the ground,
    When freedom for men, on earth must be found?
    Why do we seek the wings of a dove
    Can freedom be – where there is no love?
    Birds of freedom – a different kind
    Living – in – the – mind.

=CHORUS=: . . . High up in the sky ...

4. Seagulls sailing through the sky –
    Raise your heads and see them fly !
    Born with freedom for the skies –
    Watch their graceful swoops and dives.
    Wings of freedom are to the birds
    Who fly up in the sky.

=CHORUS=: . . . High up in the sky ...

FINALE

Wings of freedom are to the birds
Who fly up in the sky.
Fly away – fly away – fly –
Wings of freedom fly...

-~~~_._~~~

Smiling Eyes

= *February 2, 1992* =
(Lyrics to a song)

Now I see her face
On a misty dawn
How can I embrace
and hold her charm –
and touch – her heart
to my own ?

Then she came one night
In a windy storm
And her smiling eyes
so soft and warm –
her eyes – they touched
my soul.

She's my dream all day
Haunting me each night ...
Memories I paint
just turn to white –
like snow – they melt
into tears.

Tears of joy – a mystery
Dream no more – said she

Dreams are clouds of time
Touch my love – said she
And her lips of wine
enchanted me –
with soft – and warm
smiling eyes.

"~~"

Flight of the Eagle

(An Ode to K)
= June 16, 1992 =
(Lyrics to a song)

There was a man, a gentle man –
You are the world, said he.
Look at yourself, and see.

And as he spoke, I heard him say –
A thousand yesterdays
Have bound you to your ways.

<u>CHORUS:</u>
Watch an eagle soaring through the sky;
See it fly and never leave a mark ...
Freedom is the way it flies.

Listen to the whisper in the wind;
Hear the song that love will sing again...
Freedom is the joy it feels – to live again.

He questioned why, one does not end
So many years – of pain,
Where sorrow still remains.

continued ...

And as I looked within his eyes
Compassion spoke, so kind –
It gently touched my mind.

CHORUS: Watch an eagle soaring...

And then this man, with passion burned –
You must be free, said he –
To see what love could be...

How could it be? I ask myself ...
This man, he speaks to me –
Freedom is love, said he.

CHORUS: Watch an eagle soaring...

~*|*~

Y O U

= *September 7, 1992* =
(Lyrics to a song)

When you hold me tenderly love
And I feel so warm in your arms –
You touch my lips, you fill my heart
With a joy – you smile
And I embrace you.

Many years I waited for you
Tears and dreams so empty so blue –
And then you came, you filled my heart
With a joy – you laughed
And I laughed with you.

Time is gone when I am with you
Every moment something is new –
You lift me up, you fill my heart
With joy – you dance
And I just watch you.

continued …

As you dance among the stars
I reach out and ask you
How am I to follow you ?

Take my hand, you whisper to me
And I see a gleam in your eyes –
It lights the stars, it fills my heart
With joy – I laugh
And you laugh with me

And I embrace you,
And I dance with you,
Dance with you …
with you …
you …

```
  /\
 /  \
 \  /
  \/
```

Ancient Dreams

= December 20, 1992 =
(Lyrics to a song)

Yesterday is on my mind –
Ancient dreams that
Paint our days like a rhyme

CHORUS:

Memories of days gone by and
Still they reach and
Bind us to yesterday.

Ancient dreams that dwell in our mind –
Memories repeating in time.

Yesterday, it calls to me –
Spinning yarns of hope
Of things to be ...

CHORUS: *Memories of days...*

Yesterday, so many years –
A million dreams that
Fail to end many tears!

continued ...

FINALE:

Memories of days gone by and
Still they reach and
Bind us to yesterday.

...

No more rhymes, no yesterday sighs –
Dream no more – be free of ties

...

No more dreams, no yesterday cries –
Sleep no more, and open your eyes!
Sleep no more, and open your eyes.

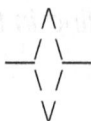

```
    /\
 __/  \__
   \  /
    \/
    V
```

ALWAYS

= *November 23, 2010* =

Each has their own field of focus for their
Particular needs and growth.
All are expressions of the Source.
And the universe is always expanding and evolving –
Always a new adventure.

And many wonderful people and teachers
that help us join the joyous adventure.
Jesus, perhaps the brightest light of all
– who knows for certain?
Buddha before him... and Lao Tse before that...
And many other lights since...

Each is part of consciousness, part of the totality.
To say that one is more right,
Or more 'in the know' than another
is to misunderstand
the many aspects of manifestation.

The great Intelligence of creation permeates all.

That which we have labeled intelligence,
– the IQ sort
– the ability to solve problems and puzzles,
Is but a minuscule portion of that totality.

continued ...

To think that the part could ever comprehend the whole
points in the direction of delusion,
And is illusion.

We are part of that whole, whether we know it or not,
whether we admit it or not.

Those who dare to explore and challenge the 'status quo'
of thought - those know what freedom is;
Those will bring innovation and a new clarity
to their field of endeavor.

Do not set out to prove that something is right or wrong,
For in either case it encourages resistance and conflict
instead of generosity and harmony.

Instead, look forward to discovering something that
might inspire joy in others.

Let not the arrogance of personal desire supersede
kindness that might be offered
when it is most welcomed.

For it is yourself that you are meeting,
in every moment,
in every way,
in every place
—Always—

wladicus – 2010.11.23

58

The Light of Joy

= *November 17, 2011* =

Not under the authority of any institution
There is freedom to explore and discover
Beyond the limitations of authority.

You are a child of freedom,
And yet you give it up so quickly -
And then the light of day is longer in coming.

As a babe, not long out of the light,
In the depth of your eyes, gleamed a spark
sublime.
And the world wanted your joy.

But the burden of the world,
Could not understand the light of joy,
And failed to see its worth.

wladicus – 2011.11.17

oOo

Section 2
ATTITUDE for CHANGE

This section records a public talk
given in May of 1987.

The talk discusses attitudes and perception that
can open one to a more meaningful
understanding and participation in life.

~ wladicus ~


```
    /\
   /  \
   \  /
    \/
```

Opening Words

When one hears the words "Philosophy of Life" several different ideas may come to mind. It is commonly understood that every person has some sort of philosophy of life, which they adhere to, based on their upbringing and the mental conditioning to which they were exposed in their early years of life.

It is inevitable that every person will have some sort of philosophy of life, or principles, by which they live and set personal goals. Many people, however, may not be aware of the fact that the life they live, the things they do and how they react to given situations are all the result of inherited tendencies and deep mental conditioning.

Most people have a vague idea that they have a certain approach to life, or maybe a philosophy. But, when they are asked to give a coherent explanation of what motivates them, and how they perceive the purpose of life, then they are lost for words. It is much easier to shrug it off and say something to the effect that it's beyond them to look into this matter of life that deeply.

And yet, we live life and in essence we are life! Therefore, should we not find out what or who we are, what we do, and why we do it? It seems to me that to live wholly, and to participate purposefully, would put one closest to being "true to oneself".

To earn a lot of money and to become financially independent may be a practical goal for mere physical existence. But, if one were to die tomorrow, then of what use is all that wealth? The energy expended in gaining it is capable of much greater revelation and manifestation.

Why are there worries and sorrows? There is despair and anxiety in the world. In the thousands of years of recorded history, man has struggled to rise to what we today call Modern Civilization. But, has he gained anything deeply valuable or new? Is he fundamentally different from the savage who huddled in his cave by a fire, wondering about the stars and fearful of what the dark may bring?

Technologically, man has soared to unbelievable heights. We have sent people to the moon and brought them home safely. Eye surgery with a laser beam would appear to be miraculous healing with instruments of light, veritable sorcery, to people of only one hundred years ago. The electronic personal computer would have been revered as a god or a wondrous spirit by denizens of the Middle Ages.

There has been much to marvel about, but there has also been much sadness. Conflict and violence seem to be an ever-present misery, as if they were a collective curse of humankind. We hear a lot of talk about peace, but war and violence, both inwardly and outwardly, have been a demonstrable reality. Even to this day, we are not rid of wars and human struggle in general.

Why is that so? To understand the situation of the world around us we must first understand what goes on within us. What I bring up here is nothing new, but too few have bothered to notice, and as a result, man is slow to grow inwardly.

Here are some phrases to reflect upon at some depth. These phrases, or sayings, have appeared in one form or another, in many great religions and philosophies, and they contain what may be thought of as the "Truth of the Ages" or wisdom:

KNOW THYSELF

AS ABOVE, SO BELOW

AS WITHIN, SO WITHOUT

DO UNTO OTHERS
AS YOU WOULD HAVE THEM DO UNTO YOU

AS A MAN THINKETH, SO IS HE

AS YOU SOW, SO SHALL YOU REAP

LET THE DEAD BURY THE DEAD

I AM THE LIFE AND THE WAY

THERE ARE MANY ROOMS IN MY FATHER'S HOUSE

IF I HAVE NOT LOVE, THEN I AM NOTHING

THERE IS ONLY ONE LIFE, NOT MANY LIVES,
AND WE ARE ALL PART OF THAT ONE LIFE

The above sayings have appeared in many different forms, on countless occasions, from several great world teachers and religions or philosophical luminaries. They address the human spirit and moral nature.

The hope for humanity's future lies in its capacity to study its own nature, to see its shortcomings, and to rise above the selfish motivations, which have driven human beings to various ca lamities since time immemorial.

Each human being is an integral part of the universe we live in. It is, therefore, incumbent upon each individual, to approach life with seriousness and sincerity, but not from any mood of gravity, or depression, or panic – but rather with a "light heart" and with utter confidence in the wisdom of creative intelligence. It would be to our great benefit to understand our relationship to life, and how we can best employ our particular talents.

Yes, we must carefully review our personal philosophies of life and see if they are meaningful to life. There are many paths or ways of attending to what we might call our "spiritual evolution".

Perhaps, if enough people become actively involved in meaningful living, then the quality of mind in the world will rise to a new height of awareness – perhaps to a level of awareness never before thought possible.

William Shakespeare once wrote:

There are more things in heaven and earth ...
than are dreamt in our philosophies.

I invite you, the reader, to take the challenge. Do some deep "soul searching" and join the few who choose to more deeply understand life.

Dr. Richard Maurice Bucke was a luminary of the 19 th century. He wrote two notable books, of which the second "COSMIC CONSCIOUSNESS" has become a well-known and widely studied work. The first book that he wrote, "Man's Moral Nature", although it is not as well known, is also a landmark work, which laid the foundation concepts for the book "COSMIC CONSCIOUSNESS". Here are two quotes from the last page of "Man's Moral Nature", which are worthy of consideration:

... religion, morality, and happiness are three names for the same thing – MORAL ELEVATION.

This, then, is the end, the conclusion of the whole matter: Love all things– not because it is your duty to do so, but because all things are worthy of your love. Hate nothing. Fear nothing. Have absolute faith. Whoso will do this is wise; he is more than wise – he is happy.

I have entitled this essay "ATTITUDE for CHANGE" because it is our attitude towards life that determines much of what appears to happen to us – to the world. It is not that the world needs change for the sake of change. That is foolish, for we have seen a lot of change as such, and it appears that we have gained nothing deeply vital from that sort of change.

Here, we are talking about change in the sense of mutation. A complete difference is implied, rather than a modification or rearrangement of human behavior. I speak not of a physical mutation as such, but perhaps what we might call a 'moral' mutation. And here, by 'moral', I do not mean 'moral' in the limited sense that it is usually defined, but 'moral' in the context of a completely unbiased universal matrix which may currently be beyond the comprehension of 'normal' human mentality.

Also the word 'ATTITUDE' as it is applied to this talk/essay, is a key here. It is our attitudes, our conditioned motivators in the deep recesses of our inherited race consciousness, that need changing, or mutation, if we are t o see and live life in a new way.

The following pages contain a talk presented to a group of "seekers" on the path to greater understanding of life. The talk was also presented to a meeting of about 88 people at an historic first 'Area Meeting' of the International On -the- Beam Club held in London, Ontario, Canada on May 8-9, 1987. On this occasion, the talk was delivered by Anthony (Tony) Borowsky who, with my approval, entitled the talk "The process of Change from Self to Cosmic".

Ultimately, this change in attitude that I am talking about, can be considered as one of several possible keys, which can open the door, which leads beyond the limited awareness of the world of self consciousness. Beyond this realm, a new way of seeing, feeling and thinking, shows itself as integral to life.

And thus I conclude these opening words, in the hope that the following short essay will inspire some people to delve into the wealth of resource available for 'self - improvement' and a general heightening of awareness of life.

Walter Dutchak
May 13, 1987
Lambeth, Ontario, Canada

---oooOOOooo---

Introduction to
"ATTITUDE for CHANGE "

When we say that we get an IDEA or a thought from SPIRIT it seems to me that what we are in essence talking about is a stimulus, or a vibration, which activates a thought, or an idea.

The thought is our own, from our own mental equipment. Humans are finite beings. That which we might call SPIRIT is not finite – it is INFINITE and ineffable.

INFINITE means what the word says – NOT FIN ITE!

Something finite can be DEFINED – it has definite (de - FINITE) limits that define it.

The INFINITE is NOT FINITE (IN here means NOT) and the INFINITE cannot be defined, although we often give some sort of metaphorical explanation of what it might me an – but still we really cannot possibly KNOW that which is infinite. It cannot be comprehended by the FINITE MIND, which is a characteristic faculty of human beings.

Therefore, to say that we get an idea from SPIRIT is not exactly correct. We perceive an energy (a vibration or vibratory energy) from the infinite or spiritual plane or dimension, so to speak, and it interacts with our sensory equipment (mainly brain) as a stimulus, which produces sensations of some sort that eventually result as an idea or a thought.

This thought appears to be a product of our mind or brain, however you wish to put it, and thus it is not directly an idea from SPIRIT or the infinite realm, but only a stimulus from that realm and the resulting idea or thought can then be unde   rstood to be our own.

This thought that we attribute as an inspiration from above is actually modified and qualified by the human interface of conditioning, and level or degree of attunement to the wholeness that we are a part of.

Thus if we can attune the human instrument to a level of finer perception and behavior that is more conducive to harmonious interaction with all that is part of life, then might it not be possible to 'see' a new heaven and a new earth – so-to-speak ? It is with this sort of idea in mind that the following essay has been written.

W. Dutchak – 1987.02.24

...000...

*** ATTITUDE for CHANGE ***

The intention of this talk is not to instruct, but rather to share some insights, which have opened one up to begin to realize something seemingly very important – something very urgent! It seems that an attitude for change is a basic prerequisite to achieving another quality of awareness: And that is the topic of my talk – ATTITUDE for CHANGE.

To begin, I wish to share with you a short verse by George Santayana:

> Our knowledge is a smoky pine
> That lights the pathway
> Across a void of mystery and dread.
> Bid then, the tender light of faith to shine
> By which alone the mortal heart is led
> Unto the thinking of the thought divine.

Santayana hints that knowledge is insufficient of itself, and that faith will lead the mortal to the divine. Whether he is right or not is not the important point here, but the bidding for an attitude for change is significant!

CHANGE is something we take very much for granted. If we take the time to carefully observe things around us, and in our very own lives, we can see that there is constant change taking place.

The obvious things we can observe are the changing seasons and the accompanying change in the envir onment; the weather, the vegetation, leaves of many

70

different colors falling from trees in the autumn; and in the spring, buds begin to blossom.

When we observe animals and people, we see that there is change in bodily features, the color of the hair, smiles, pouts, and of course the thing we all try to avoid talking about – aging. These are all physical changes – things that we can see. There are also changes in mood, in feelings, and changes in thinking.

By some very, very close and careful observation, we may be able to notice that in a peculiar way, all the physical changes that we observe, and all of the changes in feeling, mood and thought that we can perceive, are somehow connected to the very process of thinking itself.

The word – PERCEIVE or PERCEPTION – is rather significant here, and we will discuss it in more detail later.

Have you ever seen something, or maybe thought that you saw something that was a certain way, but then it was brought to your attention that it was not so? Then, upon close r observation, you saw, or perceived that in fact, it was not as you had thought it to be but indeed, it was different from what you were sure you saw. This is a somewhat common occurrence, and it points out a very important aspect related to our perception, or awareness of the FACT, or the nature of things.

The very point to note in this case, is, that we THOUGHT that we saw something a certain way. A THOUGHT, a CONCEPT, was operating our mental equipment, and this impeded the faculty of perception or the CLEAR SEEING of the fact. In effect, we projected our thought, or concept of the thing we were supposed to see, and saw only that which we had already been conditioned to see.

CONDITIONED THINKING

This is the fundamental principal of a prejudiced – that is, pre-judging mind. Such a mind operates from fixed concepts, which are organized sets of thoughts – or simply, a thinking pattern.

An example of conditioned thinking may be illustrated in a situation when one meets someone new. One is introduced to this new person, they chat for a while, and then it seems that one formulates an impression (a concept) of what this person is like. What is that IMPRESSION?

It is the information that is *impressed* upon the mind. The information that one has gathered about the new person gets recorded somewhere, possibly somehow on the brain cells. (Who knows for certain how this happens). Then somehow, this information organizes such that particular neural connections are established, and this forms a thinking pattern, or *concept*.

The exact mechanics may be different from what we have hypothesized, and I now suspect that it all may happen in the quantum mechanical realm of the new physics, but this is really not relevant to this discussion. The point to note is that based often on first impressions only, most people **habitually** tend to form impressions or thinking patterns – which in essence become a CONCEPT that **defines** or *judges* who or what they have encountered.

Such a concept becomes a convenience in formulating thoughts, which in effect define the world we perceive. If you understand this habitual process of concept forming or conceptualization, what would you expect happens the next time one encounters a person they have met on a previous occasion ?

Following the logic of what has been explained above, something akin to the following would most likely happen:

> The sight of him or her, triggers a particular concept, or thought pattern, by association − i.e. seeing this person again activates the associated memory of a pr evious encounter with this person. The mind at this point is engaged with the memory of previous impressions rather than the actual data of the current encounter.

Now, if one is not perceptive to the facts of the moment, then one might immediately hear a voice in one's head saying perhaps something like the following:

> For a male: "Ah yes! This is the outspoken fellow, the one who thinks he knows it all." − or, for a female: "Oh yes, this is the lady who smiles a lot, Maryna, I think. Yes, she's so proud of her jewelry and thinks that she's an authority on the behavior of men."

Can you see what is happening in these cases? THOUGHT is our master! It projects an image for our observation, based strictly on what was remembered from a first meeting impression. If we are not perceptive of this, if we cannot see this at the very moment that it is happening in our thought processes, then we are blind to the facts of that moment and do not really see that person as they really are at that moment. We only see a projection of the mind has construed to be real.

The above story is an example of conditioned thinking. People change moment to moment. Creation goes on, and we may be blind to it. If we react to previously stored thoughts, ideas, or impressions of things, encounters or situations, then we are not living in the present, in the NOW!. In fact if the aforementioned is true, then we are living in the PAST!– in TIME. Memory is simply the storehouse of past experiences and impressions. And we surely know, that logically, the past is already dead, and its information is limited, and therefore incapable of producing anything new.

We often hear it said – "Don't cry over spilt milk". – because it's gone, it's dead, and it is of no more value for the present. One should understand that in this discussion we are talking of the psychological realm of human experiencing and not the practical realm where memory is useful in such areas as science, medicine, cooking, driving, remembering where you live and your telephone number, and so on. That is not our current area of exploration. We are exploring that so-called reality projected by the conditioned habits of mind, the psychological pseudo-reality where the "self" resides, which most people assume to be the only reality and often find themselves as victims of their own mental projections.

Considering this psychological realm of the human being, thought seems to often sabotage the very good intentions of its own making, not realizing that it is living in its own illusions and thinking of them as the only reality. There is no potential for creation, or personal creativity by relying on the past, on thought.

Thought can only invent, that is, thought is capable of making or producing something different (that is to say something modified) from something already known, and therefore, the results of thought can never bring about a fundamental change, but only a revision, an improvement of sorts, or a more or less efficient or effective way of doing or explaining things. In life the compassionate intelligence of heart is always greater than the arrogant or negligent intelligence coming via the brain.

To really change something, it must be done at the very root, the origin – otherwise it is a superficial change, which amounts to the same thing in different clothing – like a WOLF IN SHEEP's CLOTHING, BUT STILL A WOLF!

DIE BEFORE YOU DIE

– or –

TO BE BORN AGAIN

If we wish to change, I mean really, sincerely *change*, from the person that we are to something totally different – to open up from one level of consciousness to another – then we must be willing – without *inner* struggle (which implies effort) – we must be willing to die unto the *old*, so as to allow the *new* to flourish.

Is there something worth dying for? – I do not mean physically. Think about it, seriously. Consider what the illumined poet Walt Whitman had to say about this matter in his master works *"Leaves of Grass"*:

> Has any one supposed it lucky to be born?
> I hasten to inform him or her it is just as lucky to die,
> – **and I know it** .

... and in another place he says:

> I am the mate and companion of people,
> all just as **immortal** and fathomless as myself,
> (They do not know how **immortal**, but I know).

The title of this talk is *"ATTITUDE for CHANGE"*.
By ATTITUDE we mean:

A DIRECTION, A COURSE, A WAY.

By CHANGE we mean:

SOMETHING TOTALLY NEW

SOMETHING THAT WAS NOT BEFORE.

Change cannot be gradual. If we put a concept of gradualness into our minds, then we are deluding ourselves, and in effect, we are always putting off until tomorrow that which should be done today. The idea of something happening *gradually* comes to us from our reluctance to give up those **good old habits** that we so dearly love and cannot bear to part with, because they are so much a part of us (i.e. of who we think and feel we are).

This is a self-defeating logic. Thought, fixed concepts, again prove to be our master by preventing change to something new. It is very difficult to convince the mental processes buy the idea of leaving our habitual comfort zone for an *unknown* .

The reason why habitual behavior has so much control over the mental processes is because it all relates back to the initial survival urge with which our species began life on this Earth. These include the inherited urges for physical survival, inherited fears related to physical survival, and all the accompanying beliefs that have been passed on over the ages from one generation to another. All of that background in one sense builds a foundation of the belief of who or what we think we are?

Do we really want to be all that past memory and belief? Is that to be our limit in life? Can we pass through those limitations of habit based on primitive urges and beliefs?

The answer is almost too simple, and yet, it is difficult to grasp, because of the very concepts that *condition* and thus *limit* our potential for life. Psychologically speaking, we are really dead to life! We live constantly in the *past* – the inherited fears and urges still have a strong hold upon us. We plan our future from those limited motivators that rule the psychological realm of our life.

The *psychological* is that which is of the PSYCHE, which is the Greek word for *soul*. There is a specific implication here, which I will discuss later on. It has a crucial link to the topic of th is talk – ATTITUDE for CHANGE.

THE PLACE OF THOUGHT

Thought has a definite, and a very valid place in our lives. Notice the word DEFINITE. It carries with it the meaning of **something that is defined**. The root word **finite** is the source of the word **definite**. Another way of gleaning the meaning of the word **definite** is to understand it to be something **defined** or **FINITE**. **FINITE** means and refers to something that is **LIMITED**.

For example, **all** knowledge is limited. If you were to have all of the available knowledge in the world at your fingertips, you may be able to rule the world, or to run a large corporate business very effectively, or come up with some very unique inventions – and that is a *practical* thing – in most cases.

However, where LIFE is concerned (i.e. that which is of the PSYCHE, the soul) – in that area **"mind"** knowledge is a very limited affair (and in a sense becomes quite impotent). Even in **practical** life (i.e. that which we put into practice or some applied use), there is always a case where the available knowledge is insufficient, and it cannot resolve problems.

Thought displays the characteristics of a mechanical and reactive function. If you carefully observe, clearly see – or perceive – the process of thinking, then it soon becomes evident that something like the following steps of activity are constantly in operation:

Through our sense organs we receive stimuli that somehow register on the brain cells.

These stimulations somehow organize in a certain pattern, through neural connections or electro-chemical/electro-magnetic, and a record is created. This record we call a memory – comparable somewhat to tape recording.

The record, or memory, can be recalled and reviewed, on demand in most cases, or by association of other stimuli that may vibrate the proper cells or a sympathetic electromagnetic resonance of some sort. (The exact detail of the process is not the important point in this analysis, just the fact that something of a fixed pattern is involved).

And so it seems that it is always a stimulation of some sort, from some source, that vibrates a certain set of brain cells or sets up a resonance that is recognized or considered to be what we call thought or thinking. As discussed above, this process of thought, is in essence, always mechanical in nature.

All thought appears to work on the principle of *re-action* – a re-action to a stimulus of some sort.

The process of thought is one of *accumulating* information (or data), and then associating, and co-relating that information, based on stimuli, to form other patterns or concepts.

From this we can see that THOUGHT is limited by what information is recorded or stored, whether it be in one person's awareness or another's. The particular ways in which that stored information is related to other information and things further adds to the limitations of thought.

It is reasonable to assume that we can "pick up" the thoughts of others, but their thoughts are fundamentally no different. The difference lies in variety rather than scope, because all thought is limited by the very nature of how they originate.

THOUGHT can be very inventive, and resourceful, for it is capable of combining into so many different patterns and concepts. BUT the invention is always the result of already known information, only it is now combined, or arranged into a NEW PATTERN with resulting new implications.

The new pattern does not increase the scope of thought. It does not make it more unlimited, but it merely presents a different application of the same old thoughts. (It has been said that there is nothing new under the sun).

What we may call NEW THOUGHT, to us personally, does not make thought new. Thought can result from various stimulations, and therefore, somebody, or some thing, already had that information in some form, and now we have recorded it and accumulated it to our own memory. We say that it is new to our experience, but in essence, it is old.

Thus one might see how a thought is a personalized view, of experience combined with beliefs and concepts of various sorts, which manifest in a certain pattern of energy flow. And a stimulus of some sort brings on this activity which we have labeled **thought**.

TWO QUESTIONS must now be carefully investigated: Where, and how, is thought to be used practically?

When is it NOT PRACTICAL, and a distinct DISadvantage to rely on thought?

It would be quite difficult, nay, not possible, in this short talk, to go into all of the details and peculiarities of how thought works, but if one wishes to pursue this avenue of investigation then modern psychology presents one logical point of view.

The process of THINKING – IMAGING – and forming CONCEPTS has been discussed, investigated and taught in many forums. To date, this does not appear to have changed the course of human thought in such a way as to result in more wholesome attitudes and a harmonious relationships between people, groups, and nations.

A brief answer to the two questions posed above would be:

1) Where and how is thought to be used practically?
   The key word here is practically. Anything PRACTICAL is that which can be put into PRACTICE.

   What do we put into practice?
      We must know how to drive a car, how to earn a living by learning a job or a profession. These are practical things.

We must know how to find our way home and it helps to remember a person's name. To learn a language to communicate would be useful, and to count your money correctly when paying for your groceries, and so on, and so on ...

All these are practical things in life, are things that we must have knowledge about in our memory, our thoughts, so that we can function properly on the physical third dimensional plane of knowledge – or we are lost.

The brain and the body are instruments designed for the expression of life on the physical plane of existence, and thoughts are the tools that are used *to order, to organize,* and to help *sustain* us so that we can enjoy a productive life experience.

Now for the second question:

2. When is it not practical, and a distinct disadvantage to rely on thought?

Here we enter the realm of the psyche or soul or that which is beyond the realm of thought. Psychologically, thought is a hindrance. It has no functional role in the life of the psyche. The rest of this talk delves deeper into the areas wher e it is most useful to transcend the unhelpful aspects of thought.

BEYOND THOUGHT-PERCEPTION

If the psyche, or the soul draws upon thought for its nourishment, then it becomes limited by the very thoughts that it holds onto as needful to its identity (actually false identity as influenced by the conditioning that influences us). The soul cannot then change, it cannot soar to greater heights of awareness. It becomes attached to the thoughts, and identifies itself with the thoughts. And thus, the soul becomes the thoughts, and an image of SELF is sustained. And SELFISHNESS or looking after self becomes the motivator.

Having only the limited realm of knowledge (i.e. thought) from which to operate, the soul does not clearly see itself in its relationship to the SOURCE of LIFE – the ONE LIFE PRINCIPLE. As a result, it becomes plagued with the consequences of identifying with thought instead. There are greed, envy, jealousy, desire, and so on – all driven and motivated by the storehouse of memory, which is thought.

So, if the soul– the psychological element – cannot live in balance based on the motivations of thought, then what is the instrument or faculty, by which it can CHANGE and become something *greater*, something *different,* something *alive* and capable of operating as ONE with the principle of LIFE (which is basically LOVE)?

The key here is **perception**. We must look at this word *perception* with some care.

There are two kinds of perception. One kind we all know about. The other, we can acquire, or uncover, and experience a *change* in consciousness.

The perception that we all know about is INTELLECTUAL perception. Based on stored knowledge, and its analysis, we *intellectualize* (i.e. use the intellect/mind/thought). And in using thought we have learned over millennia to relate various factors involved in a situation, and also we have developed an ability to discern what we call *facts*, and the resulting product would be called INTELLECTUAL PERCEPTION.

In essence, this intellectual perception is the understandin g of the relationships between certain facts, and the resulting implications. Based on this formula, we as individuals and as a species have determined our actions (in reality *re-actions*) to various problems or situations that needed our attention and a response of some sort. This is intellectual perception, which is the logical reaction to thought stimuli .

Intellectual perception has served us fairly well. One might say that it is a type of learned intelligence that humans have developed to help in early survival needs of the species. It has, in many ways, placed us 'above' other members of the animal kingdom, but now that we are beyond the basic ancient survival needs of the species, there is no significant need to totally rely on only intellectual perception for our day -to - day needs.

In fact, in appears to be evident historically, that when we are unable to detach ourselves from limiting beliefs and ingrained fears of various sorts, then we often react very disadvantageously by engaging in reactionary "defensive" or "offensive" ventures which are generally known as WARS and various other social CONFLICT. As mentioned earlier in this talk, the thought process still definitely has its place in our lives but it is deeply lacking where a more mature and insightful approach is required.

This now opens the door to look at an aid towards the maturation of human behavior. This would be in the context of the *other kind* of PERCEPTION, which can be acquired. It is a perception NOT born of thought, whereas the intellectual kind of perception *is* born of thought. Therefore, this new perception is NOT a reactionary process as is the case with thought and intellect.

It is the perception of CLEAR SEEING. We might call it **"essential"** perception, since it springs from the ESSENCE OF THE BEING of which we are holistically a part and visa versa.

This essential perception is NOT of the mind, which would be make it a product of thought, which it is not. Essential seeing might be described as CLEARLY SEEING the fact of the moment, every moment, moment-by-moment. It could be metaphorically compared to the way we breathe moment-by-moment to sustain physical life, but in this case it is a comprehensive seeing from the heart and not from the mind.

This CLEAR SEEING is learning in action. It has been referred to as a seeing "from the heart", or the essence of

Being. From this point of essential perception, there is no choice, since thought is not involved, and therefore, all action from this point of perception is what in the EAST has been called RIGHT ACTION, and not a RE-ACTION resulting from analysis by thought.

Thought may record the event that just occurred in a past moment, but this essential perception sees clearly what IS, and not the way thought records it to be from its con ditioned and biased perspective.

If one can see clearly, perceive essentially, the fact of every moment, moment-by-moment, then one enters a state of what one might call *true aliveness*. Many people have felt such a moment of exhilaration, or 'peak experience', or 'high' at some point in their life experience and this was mainly due to the fact that at that moment they were not reacting to thoughts or preconceived notions of reality.

During this process the mind is quiet, but it is very alert. There is a great difference between a **BUSY MIND** and an **ALERT MIND** .

There is much to discuss and contemplate on this topic, but that would be the subject of another work. So, I will briefly summarize as follows:

> Essential perception can be likened to a sort of direct **WITNESSING** and experiencing the movements in life (of which we are an integral part). By opening to this essential perception there is a direct experiencing without the often

confusing and painful interference of limited concepts or thoughts.

TO BE OR NOT TO BE ...

In the early part of this talk, I asked whether it would be possible to pass through the limitations imposed by conditioned thinking. Then I said that the answer is almost too simple, and yet it is difficult to grasp, because of the very concepts that condition and limit our potential for a greater expression of Life.

In fact the question amounts to Hamlet's quandary (from Shakespeare's play Hamlet):

"TO BE or Not TO BE   "

Metaphorically speaking from a psychological aspect, we are dead to creative "being" if thought alone is our driver (controller/decision maker/motivator/reactor).

In most cases, when we live emotionally from the thought realm then we behave as mere automatons, or robots, with significant psychological disturbances such as envy, greed, love/hate, and all the rest of those common motivators that have conditioned, and driven humanity for thousands upon thousands of years.

Much has been learned and said about the HUMAN aspect in the phrase "HUMAN BEING", and all our learning a nd purpose tends to propel us into the "doing" aspect of life. What about "being"? "TO BE OR NOT TO BE? That is the question."   Are we ready for a new birth?

In the thousands of years of recorded history of mankind, humans have not changed fundamentally − at the root − .

People still have fears, and are driven by urges. Envy and greed have not left us, and there is much sorrow. To this very day, humans are still at war with each other, both 'within' and 'without'. This brings to mind an ancient wisdom saying – AS WITHIN, SO WITHOUT– or its twin saying – AS ABOVE , SO BELOW.

On another note, one can see that there have been great and worthy achievements, and there have been fantastic advances in technology, but deep within, at the root (radical), the soul still struggles. It struggles and searches for the answer to its miseries. All this points in the direction of a radical transformation for the solution.

Because a transformation is always possible, there is hope. Not the hope that is bred of fear (by thought) – for that would be a very limited hope, and it would be prone to suffer more sorrowful disappointments.

NO! There is a hope, that a radical transformation of human behavior is possible through essential perception and grace. Grace is another topic of discussion that will not be covered here, but it is intertwined with the action of complete surrender to the power that is integral to our being (God, Spirit, Consciousness, the Over Soul, etc.– it has been called by many names).

The finite mind cannot say anything of real value about these concepts, but with essential perception the heart will communicate all that needs to be known when it is required.

BEYOND CONCEPTUAL REALITY

When we become slaves to the workings of the mind, then a perceptual 'blindness' to the reality of life ensues. Thus we become trapped in **CONCEPTUAL REALITY**, which is based on knowledge. Consciousness continues to manifest at a limited level, a level with the inherent limitations knowledge of the mind always has.

To say that – "I will work on it...", and gradually eliminate such impediments as envy, for example, and then to believe that this will manifest less envy than previously, is a misleading concept. If I have less envy, then I still have envy, and – here is the main point of all this – **I AM THAT ENVY WHEN I EXPRESS IT**, because at that moment, there is **NOTHING** but **ENVY** expressing, and I therefore must be that envy. This envy then gains strength as a working concept **EVERY TIME** it is expressed or entertained. So, **GRADUALLY** won't do it. The same habit, condition or behavior rebuilds and reasserts itself.

To be rid of envy, for example, I must see it for what it is, and I must clearly see how it operates in my experience (of life), in my thoughts, and in my actions. I must see it at the very moment that it begins to stir. And then, at that moment of clear seeing, when I see it for what it really is, which is what **I AM EXPRESSING AT THAT MOMENT**, and I see the consequences of its expression – BEFORE it expresses – THEN, at that moment there is a release from envy, or whatever the limiting behavior happens to be.

This in essence amounts to a process of NEGATION. It is a practice of NOT giving expression to detrimental thoughts, feelings or actions, by SEEING them clearly for what they are. Essential perception is in the domain of consciousness that is beyond conceptual reality. It is a domain of ACTION rather than reaction.

It has been said that THE EYES ARE THE WINDOWS OF THE SOUL, and ESSENTIAL PERCEPTION, is in essence, an eye, a window through which a CLEAR SEEING is experienced.

LOVE HAS NO OPPOSITE

Can we change our attitude of life, towards life, in life? It is really a change of self and not a change TOWARDS , or OF, or IN anything specifically– because we are integral to life. Therefore the question can be simply put – CAN WE CHANGE ?

If thought– the mind – is the MOTIVATOR, the DRIVER – then we encounter experiences based on reactions to conditioned thinking and beliefs. This approach (through thought) results in a conceptual life, the "DREAM" (LEELA) we live.

Essential perception finds one awakening from that dream of limitation and into full awareness of being and love.

A twentieth century philosopher of life (and spiritual teacher), J. Krishnamurti, expressed his perception of LOVE as follows:

Love is its own eternity;
it is the real,
the supreme,
the immeasurable.

The prime mover is LOVE, TRUTH, THE IMMEASURABLE and it is the essence of reality. It is beyond the grasp of intellect. It is GOD, SPIRIT, AWARENESS ITSELF – or whatever name you wish to give it; but the name or idea, or concept, is still not IT because it is beyond conceptualizing, beyond mind, and beyond intellect. It transcends all of these, it is INEFFABLE . We can only

94

point to it metaphorically, with limited concepts, inspired words, and instructive parables. It is pure LOVE – that which we all seek as humans and that which constitutes us as BEING .

This LOVE is the essence and being of all. Because the very nature of thought is dualistic (i.e. characterized by opposites – good,/bad, love/hate, hot/cold, etc.), we fail to comprehend this INEFFABLE LOVE and often connect it for the dualistic mental opposite – hate. The kind of love that is opposite to hate (the dualistic kind), is limited (and of the mind). It is just as limited, and finite as hate, and therefore it is NOT this INEFFABLE LOVE .

Love as described in many sacred scriptures, can be felt to be that supreme, immeasurable love, the motivator of life. That kind of love HAS NO OPPOSITE! It is a non-dualistic love. It is not the love of the market place. IT CANNOT HAVE AN OPPOSITE! – for it is of INFINITE capacity.

LOVE can always comprehend hate, and by so doing, this LOVE compassionately enfolds hate, and takes away its sting: But hate can never comprehend LOVE, this LOVE which is of the UNITY aspect of LIFE. Hate can only know itself and the thoughts of memory which feed it.

William Shakespeare, who really seemed to understand the character of the human mind, puts it this way in one of his v erses:

Love is not love
Which alters when it alteration finds,

Or bends with the remover, to remove.
O, No! It is an ever -fixed mark,
That looks on tempests and is never
shaken.

I mentioned before that in the thousands of years of recorded history of humankind, there is no evidence of a fundamental change in the violent and sorrowful nature of human beings as a whole. Nevertheless, we have just had a peek at love, hope, and compassion, of which the dualistic mind is not directly aware.

We have many records from illumined sources that brought and continue to bring the message of unity love and awareness to a world in sorrow and pain and hungry for change.

Pierre Teilhard de Chardin has envisioned in his work "The Phenomenon of Man", that the eventual result of human spiritual evolution will lead to a NEW consciousness on a global scale, which he calls the NOOSPHERE.

Chardin was a Catholic priest, and a scientist disciplined in anthropology in the early twentieth century. His vision and writings crossed the "boundaries" of the limited thought and dogma of the religious systems of his era and thus he was suspended from his clerical position and he was forbidden to publish his works.

However, after his death, his family and those who saw the potential in the revelations of his vision, published all of his works. The world, (i.e. those in the world who saw the value of his works) responded with enthusiastic pursuit of understanding what he had to share.

Today, Pierre de Chardin's works are even taught in Catholic seminaries – one of the many paradoxes that seem to appear in our experience of life.

The point is that the dedication and work of people like Chardin are just a small example of the various manifestations of LOVE. His work points to the possible road that humans can take, that they can change.

All the great teachings seem to be about change towards greater potential and expression of life. Such teachings often include changing the base character and behavior of "unconscious" humans by removing the "veils" that cloud our vision and thus "awaken" us to consciousness – to a life more abundant (John 10:10 ... "that they might have life, and that they might have it more abundantly").

COMMUNICATING
the ATTITUDE for CHANGE

It appears that not everyone receives the same message, seemingly a hidden message, but one might say that it is hidden in plain sight. Perhaps it is just misunderstood, or not essentially perceived. Is there an inherent limitation in verbal communications?

Thoughts, and therefore concepts, are limited – no matter how big and all-encompassing they may be. Our ability to communicate ideas with clarity is always a challenge for the dualistic mind. We use words, and words are only symbols made up of other symbols called letters or characters. These symbolic representations are then used to paint a symbolic "mind picture" which we assume will be understood by everyone in the same way that we see it.

Have you ever tried to explain something that you vividly saw and understood deeply, to another person, even to a close friend, or to your spouse? What is it that most often seems to happen in this situation?

After you have finished relating what you want to say, you find that it is not exactly how it happened, or how you saw and felt it. Often you cannot find the words to express what you feel and know to be a reality.

The word is NEVER the thing itself. The word is but a mere symbol representing the fact, and it can never equal the fact. And then there is the possibility that one misperceived what was seen or heard and so the retelling of it is still not clear.

The above might give you an idea how great world spiritual teachers may have encountered significant difficulty in relating their teachings. Although the teaching may be transmitted at a high level of awareness, the learning is usually received on the intellectual level.

Intellectual perception of the message, is the limiting factor. It has been said that the *intellects* cannot inherit the "Kingdom of Heaven". Probably because they know too much – in a limiting sense. Their knowledge limits and interferes with CLEAR SEEING or ESSENTIAL PERCEPTION .

AS TO THE CHANGE

The foregoing material, in one sense, has been a pre-amble, to two main factors as identified by the words ATTITUDE and CHANGE.

As long as one tries to understand life with intellectual knowledge only, then that is all that one has to rely on – the limitations of intellectual knowledge (which is thought). This knowledge is always prone to error, misinterpretation, assumptions, changes and erroneous conclusions.

It is not my intention to tell you a story. Nor do I pretend to teach you   for no one can do that but yourself, through what one might call the "inner" aspects of being.   But, I wish to sincerely share my insights, though they may be imperfect and limited, with others who find in themselves a similar urgency.

It is my conviction that an ATTITUDE for CHANGE contains at least one of the keys to clearer revelation of life. Without significant change in attitude about life or oneself, how can we even begin to resolve the conundrums of human behavior?

What is ATTITUDE?

Attitude is a course, a direction, or a way.
And CHANGE is always from one thing to something totally different.

Change in this sense can be understood as a mutation. Mutation is not an evolution from one thing to another. Evolution always builds on something existing, and modifies it to adapt to varying conditions.

On a physical level we may see evolution. Unlike evolution, mutation is an abrupt change from one thing to something totally different. There is no gradual change – no sense of gradation – in mutation.

An organic mutation is the sudden change that occurs to the cell and its genetic code. With the code changed, it is now something new. What we would consider to be a negative or undesirable form of mutation would be something like the disease we call cancer in its various forms. A positive mutation might be a change in brain cell structure that introduces a new quality of mind, perhaps.

Where then, does the attitude come from? Basically, the attitudes that 'control' or influence our lives are the conditioning factors, the fixed concepts and urges that motivate us to think and do things the way that we do them.

A well renowned poet from Lebanon, Kahlil Gibran, insists that we must be rid of these limiting attitudes, and change to the higher nature.

In the following words Kahlil Gibran gives us a hint metaphorically, of a 'spirit that envelops the earth'. Here he confidently proclaims the power in living with freedom from fixed concepts:

You are not enclosed within your bodies,
nor confined in houses and fields.

That which is you dwells above the mountain
and roves with the wind.

It is not a thing that crawls into the sun for warmth
or digs holes into darkness for safety,

But a thing free, a spirit that envelops the earth
and moves in the ether.

KNOW THYSELF

When life sends us a "wake-up call" we may wish to pursue the study and understanding of life and our relationship to it. We begin to learn about ourselves and the world through the intellectual route – using thought and concepts. That is how we are brought up and conditioned by our cultures and in our school systems.

If there comes upon us a burning desire to be truly free – free of the limitations that seem to plague our experiences in life, then we may be 'pushed' to change. Our attitudes will undergo a perceptual change. Then, as our sincerity, commitment, and our intensity to knowing ourselves moment-by-moment increases, then we start to perceive from a different level.

Somehow, perhaps by our intensity and grace, we begin to truly comprehend with an **ESSENTIAL PERCEPTION**. To comprehend the essence of what we are at the root or at the 'heart' of being, to know ourselves in that way is beyond the capacity of conceptual thinking.

To KNOW ABOUT oneself is very different than to KNOW ONESELF "inside out" so-to-speek. To know oneself timelessly – moment-by-moment.

Knowing about oneself is intellectualizing. It is a matter of inventing and maintaining an identity based on cultural conditioning, likes and dislikes, preferences, opinions, education, and so on.

Knowing Oneself (not about oneself) is in a sense really living what one *is*, from the aspect of ONE LIFE – and there the 'personal self' cannot go.

The personal self has so many bundles of attachments to greed, envy, hate, selfishness, and comparison. It is opinionated and judgmental and generally separative (i.e. making a distinction between me and the world, me and the 'other', me and not me).

All of these are conflicting manifestations of the dualistic experience of life. A non-dualistic view was expressed by J. Krishnamurti in his book "I AM THE WORLD", where he detailed a beautiful way of seeing life anew and left us with the deeply meaningful statement which points to a deeply psychological if not spiritual understanding of our relationship to life. The statement which he often repeated throughout his lectures was:

I am the world, and the world is me.

Inevitably, a new attitude, a new direction, results in change. The limitations of thought find their proper place in practical applications of daily life.

By understanding/seeing the limitations of thought, the **human** aspect of the human being is relieved of mental suffering. No longer encumbered by conceptual reality, the **being** aspect manifests in symphony with the **human** aspect , as an expression of wholeness.

The ONE life is limitless, all powerful, and the ONLY FACT and REALITY. It expresses through all of its manifestations and the human being with self knowledge sees that its very life is THAT LIFE.

This is the ATTITUDE of INTELLIGENCE of the ONE LIFE. Only from such an attitude can change occur, real CREATION, moment-by-moment, and every moment is NOW.

This is the realm of the INFINITE, the ETERNAL, which means that which is of NO TIME. Time is the invention or perception of thought. ESSENTIAL PERCEPTION points to infinity and is of   NO-TIME .

In its endless, disorderly chatter, the third dimensional mind (thought) plays endless games of power struggle. It has desires to re-live pleasurable moments of the past, and it is haunted by fears of what the future may bring.

This mind is caught up in its own selfish struggles, and the resulting pains and pleasures, joys and sorrows. It cannot accept, nor can it perceive that all of LIFE is ONE.

The mind will theorize, intellectualize and play many '*games of life*'. But, this mind cannot hide its nature and its limitations to one who has awakened from that DREAM of individualized   personal self.

The ATTITUDE for CHANGE starts with dispassionately observing the movement and mechanism of thought as a witness aware of the manifestation of thought. That sets the attitude or position from which change is accessible.

From such a position one is not '*mesmerized*' or captivated by the workings of thought and thus **ESSENTIAL PERCEPTION** brings light to the witnessing of the activities of mind.

Then change is inevitable, for one 'sees' the limitations and the inhibitions, but not from a place of thought where things are measured and compared and then decisions and choices are made.

Now that one is free of the machinations of thought, the obvious course, the needed change ensues, without intellectual choice.

There is no choosing when essential perception is the guide. Where limited and conflicting thought no longer interferes, RIGHT ACTION abides.

Walter Dutchak 1987.02.22
edited 2013.05.13

Section 3
My Yesterday

These words provide a glimpse
of my yesterday
as I could best express it
in the songs that I wrote
from 1966 to 1977

~ Roses ~
2001.10.16

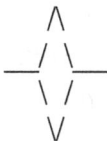

```
      /\
  _ /  \ _
    \  /
      \/
```

REMEMBERING MEMORIES

I see a lovely sunset
     calling a sweet goodnight to me;
I hear a tiny bluebird
     singing with its head high to me;
I feel a sadness of a happy time
     remembering memories –
Our love and laughter under the apple tree,
     remembering memories.

Sunny, funny faces on the beachside
     as we walked hand in hand;
Love letter traces filled with kisses
     we wrote one Sunday in the sand.
I felt a funny feeling down deep inside
     remembering memories –
Oh, and that walk we took that rainy day,
     remembering memories.

CHORUS:

Oh I do remember
That long and cold September
When loneliness came endlessly.

My time for love had faded
And I have since then waited;
Just how long will it be?

continued …

I see a lovely sunrise peeking,
  saying good morning to me.
I hear some baby bluebirds crying
  for love and warmth to me.
I guess the word would be goodbye,
  but those remembering memories
Are what he left behind the day he died –
  remembering memories.

I'm remembering memories.

—x—

SUMMER SOUNDS

The sky was blue and now I'll tell you
how it used to be,
As we sat there, around that old oak tree.

Oh how we loved the smell of dew drops
That fell on green grass –
those summer mornings.

<u>CHORUS:</u>
We loved to walk
when the sun was down,
Across the land
with bare feet on cold ground,
And stop and listen
to the summer sounds.

And when the sky was blue, we fell in love
Under that old oak tree with the sun above.
Oh, how the birds sang us a song of love –
We thanked God above for our summer love.

CHORUS: We loved to walk ...

My mama said that's not the way it should be,
And the time will come and then
you both will see.
This summer love won't last forever,
'Cause love is never a moment's glory.

CHORUS: We loved to walk ...

—/\—

I Love Thee

Why do I love you and want you night and day?
My soul can reach you in a hundred different ways.
I love thee with a smile, tears, and all my breath;
And I shall love thee even better after death.

Why do I want you by sun and candlelight?
Love, peace and forgiving, you turn the heavens bright.
I love thee with a smile, tears, and all my breath;
And I shall love thee even better after death.

Oh yes, oh yes, I need you like the sun
that needs the sky;
I can't live without you
and here is the reason why –

Because I love thee with a smile, tears,
and all my breath;
And I shall love thee even better
after death.

___--**--___

Cold Like the Wind

Oh how cold the wind can blow,
Like fear of death, that shows
when someone's dying –
Like you my love.

How like stone he can be –
A thousand trees can crush me,
But not hurt me like your love
that hurt me –
When you set me free.

Oh how cold the wind can blow,
Like fear of death, that shows
when someone's dying –
Like you my love.

A roar of thunder echoed
with the wind;
I stood by his grave – terror within!

My tears fell on cold cheeks
that once were kissed by him;
And now I'm lonely and cold –
like the wind!

*_oOo_*

The Secret of Life

I know why some people love each other,
I know how some people get along together.

CHORUS:
You can't buy it from me oh-no-no,
You'll have to find out for yourself –
That's what they call the secret of life.

Do you know why people try to help each other
And do you know why soldiers fight
and kill their brothers?

CHORUS: **You can't buy it from me ...**

Do you know why we are here with each other,
And do you know where we will go
when it's all over?

CHORUS: **You can't buy it from me ...**

...+++...

What's the Use of Living

**Life for you is phony
and its hard to find your way.
Listen to me only –
to what I have to say:**

CHORUS:
What's the use of living if you can't
have any fun;
What's the use of loving if you can't
love everyone?
Life is worth living, and I'm off
to giving it a try.

**People work all day and night;
People work for bread and light,
Some for money and some for fun;
Listen to me everyone.**

CHORUS: What's the use of living ...

**Have you heard what people say,
"Smile a while, you'll be OK"?
That is said for you and me –
Live your life, oh can't you see?**

CHORUS: What's the use of living ...

==###==

Is It Love?

Is it love that hits your heart
When you just don't know what to do?
You sit and think, and wander far,
And wonder why you feel so blue.

Is it love that makes you weak,
And so you wish and kiss each star?
You don't know what you want to seek,
And yet you know it's oh so far!

Is it love when dreams come true,
Just for the moment – then they're gone?
You ask the moon if he loves you,
And wait all night to see the dawn.

Is it love, that passionate kiss
That makes you feel you want him more?
You tell yourself "Love, I can't miss!"
And live and hope, close by its shore.

Is it love that makes you wait
To touch his face, just once again?
If a million stars will say he's late,
Will love still keep you loving him?

...~...

Did You Ever ?

Did you ever want a friend
For yourself, not just to lend;
A special one, so you can spend
Just one night – that'll never end?

Did you ever really love
Something sent from up above;
Made your own heart really spin,
And you kept saying – you love him?

Did you ever have a dream
That made you happy – so it seemed;
And when you found it was not real,
Do you know how bad it feels?

Did you ever know someone
That made you think 'the good he's done'?
All the good old days you had,
And wished for more – that made you sad?

Did you ever really love,
Filled with spirit from above?
Do you ever want to say –
You love him – day by day?

;-) :-) :-(:-o o-:)-: (-: (-;

Sands of Yesterday

See the sands of yesterday –
A time of romance was yesterday.
The nightingale, she sang her song,
She sang it loud, she sang it long –
Today, like yesterday.

See the sands of yesterday –
Hear them laugh at yesterday.
The moon and stars they shine their light,
They shine it loud and long each night –
Today, like yesterday.

Live, laugh and love – be strong.
Memories will come along and go away –
Today, like yesterday.

See the sands of yesterday –
We look back on yesterday.
A time of peace, a time of war,
What are we still looking for –
Today, like yesterday?

-&&&-

Recipe for Happiness

One meadow of happiness,

Prepare it the way you like the best,
sprinkled with summertime.
For added color, now add a flower,
make sure it's well combined.

Handful of faith, a cup of give and take
as soon as you can.
Put this together, add different weather
from time to time.

A pinch of laughter, now and hereafter
will keep it fresh.
Now add a song, make it just one,
the one you like the best.

Now ice it all with love,
sprinkled from above as you can see.
All this you combine, and cook it with time,
as happy as can be.

As happy as can be – as happy as can be...

_.=-=-=-=-=-=._

Happiness My Way

Sweet wine and the sun
Rise light to everyone.
A taste of new born day
Is happiness my way.

A whisper of a sound
And soon you'll be housebound
To fly across the sea –
Is happiness for me.

CHORUS:
For life is sweet and time is gentle;
Seasons follow – years – and I know
Gazing at the sunset each day
Tears and happiness come my way.

And you feel around you,
Love and warmth astound you;
It's then I have to say
It's happiness my way.

CHORUS:
For life is sweet and time is gentle;
....

__ooO0Ooo__

It Came Naturally

Long time ago
There were two simple people,
Each loving with an equal glow;
And let me tell you:

'Twas a happy time –
They loved the birds and flowers,
Possessed each living fruit and tree;
It came naturally.

And it was long ago-
They watched the sea by moonlight,
Loved every leaf and had plenty;
It came naturally.

Then there came a time they had temptation –
Every hour took some sun away.
It was time to run away and start anew;
And through the sun there came a cloudy day.

But that was long ago.
Now we are simple people,
Still loving with an equal glow –
And let me tell you:

It's a happy time –
We love the birds and flowers,
Possess each living fruit and tree;
It came naturally.

>>>0<<<

My Yesterday

Tomorrow will be yesterday,
The years will pass, the sun will stay.
I walk the land, the hills today,
And kiss the shore where you once stood –
　　... yesterday.

Tomorrow will come every day,
And time will tell of yesterday;
O summer kisses, quiet nights,
And lullabies were new, are old –
　　... yesterday.

　　Years will pass everyday,
　　Time stays young but we grow gray.

I still see my yesterday.
People will die but this land will stay.
This land will stay day to day,
And live tomorrow, but I will be –
　　... yesterday.

—}*{—

Rippling Waters

Rippling waters from a brook
go gently down to rocks and sands
and go astray;
To other rocks and other waters
moving gently to the shore
and is kissed away.

Rippling, dancing, singing waters
move around and touch the seashells
in different ways.
And then the moon will sprinkle stardust,
and make love to rippling waters
until it's day.

Love has created and born a scenery.
This love – you can't hide it,
It's there for all to see –
It's there for all to see.

On a hill I see below me,
rippling waters moving slowly to the sea,
Seeking for a breath of life,
from the moon that's in the night –
How can this be?

But God has created and born a scenery.
This love – you can't hide it,
It's there for all to see –
It's there for you and me

--->>>.<<<---

That's Life

Time won't stand still
'cause I'm singing this song
Bluebirds will sing when winter is gone.
Babies will cry – and
People will die
and
I'll keep singing ... that's life ... that's life.

Children always fight
and folks are in a hurry.
Roses will bloom and dogs will get dirty.
Bad boys will try – and
Lovers will sigh
and
I'll keep singing ... that's life ... that's life.

Night will draw near,
Stars will keep shining.
Somehow, somewhere, I will be dying.
I'll wonder why – and
Then say goodbye
but 'til then
I'll keep singing ... that's life ... that's life.

~~}{~~

Blue-Green Mountain

I walk by the blue-green mountain,
I gaze at the ice-clear sea;
Yes it's here by the blue-green mountain,
It's here that I feel free.

> It's here by the green,
> Where my shadow isn't seen,
> And the time of day isn't gone.

I walk by the green, soft meadow
Where the sun shines down at me.
I look at the sky above me –
At the thought of heaven, I feel free.

Oh I see the world around me,
And I know this earth isn't free;
But I still walk by the blue-green mountain,
And I know that it's here that I feel free.

---<[}{]>---

ALWAYS

How many times will a star twinkle in the night?
How many times will the blue heavens light?
How many golden moons will it take 'til he knows
I love him --- always?

How many drops of rain will fall from the sky?
How many rainbows will I see before he's mine?
But how many times will I hope to see him
And I love him --- always.

CHORUS: *It will take a thousand teardrops,*
It will take a hundred times,
It will take me pretty flowers,
Fifty million different kinds –
But I love him --- always.

How many people will I pass along the way?
How many children will I see, who laugh and play?
How many babies will I see, that won't be mine?
But I love him --- always.

How many times will I get on my knees
                                and say a prayer?
How many times will I keep saying that I care?
And how many hearts will he break to pieces?
But I love him --- always.

_...-+-..._

To Be Free

I see a little bird flying swiftly,
High above mountains,
Way across the sea,
Far away through eternity –
This little bird flies
To be free.

If I was a little bird, I'd fly swiftly
High above mountains,
Way across the sea;
I'd fly away to heaven and say –
I'm a little bird who flies
To be free.

But I'm not a little bird, but I'm free –
Free to do anything that's good for me.
I'm not a little bird
who flies through eternity,
But I'm a little girl who sings
To be free.

-o()o-

When Will We Ever Learn

Where does all the starlight come
This late evening?
Where does all the starlight come
This early morn?
Where does all the starlight come
That's up there, in heaven above?
When will we ever learn? (2 times)

How come the birds sing their song
This early morning?
How come the birds sing their song
This summer day?
How come the birds sing their song,
Where does their song come from?
When will we ever learn? (2 times)

How come I can sing a song
This early morning?
How come I can sing a song
This early day?
How come I can sing a song,
How does this all come along?
When will we ever learn? (2 times)

olo

A Friend of Mine

= *Thursday, June 2, 1977* =

Give a kiss and a simple wish,
Take a summer walk
    with a friend of mine,
Maybe talk and have some wine,
    together.

Magic moonlight in the cornfield,
Take a walk in the summertime,
Maybe talk with a friend of mine,
    forever.

Give a little for a moment,
Come and sit with a friend of mine.
Don't you cry, you'll be fine, together.

Just for a moment − take a little
Give some loving to a friend of mine.
Take a rainbow − last forever,
Be with me and a friend of mine,
Be with me and a friend of mine.

Painted hours and pretty flowers,
Take them all to a friend of mine.
You will love a friend of mine,
    forever.

-~ . ~-
V

ARE YOU ?

= 1999 =

Are you listening ?
Are you smiling ?
Are you thinking ?
Are you - are you ?
Are you, you   ?